SCHOLASTIC FIRST DISCOVERY

Whales

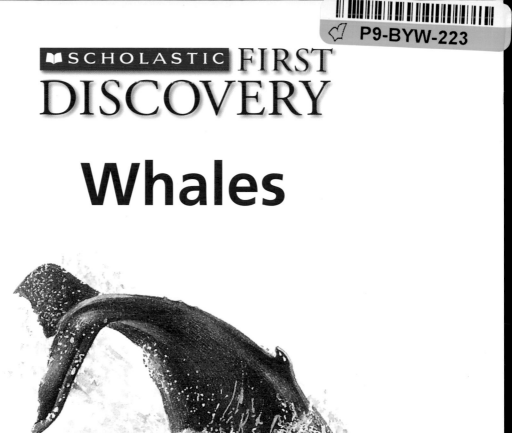

Created by Gallimard Jeunesse,
Claude Delafosse, Ute Fuhr, and Raoul Sautai
Illustrated by Ute Fuhr and Raoul Sautai

SCHOLASTIC REFERENCE
an imprint of

SCHOLASTIC

Whales are incredible animals!

Whales live in the sea. But they are not fish. They are mammals. Mammals breathe air and give their babies milk. Fish do not.

Whales have two flippers
and a large tail.

The biggest whale
is the blue whale.
It is more than 90 feet long!

Pilot whale

Porpoise

There are two kinds of whales — whales with
teeth and whales with baleen instead of teeth.
These are toothed whales.
They use their teeth to eat big animals,
such as octopuses, sharks, and squid!

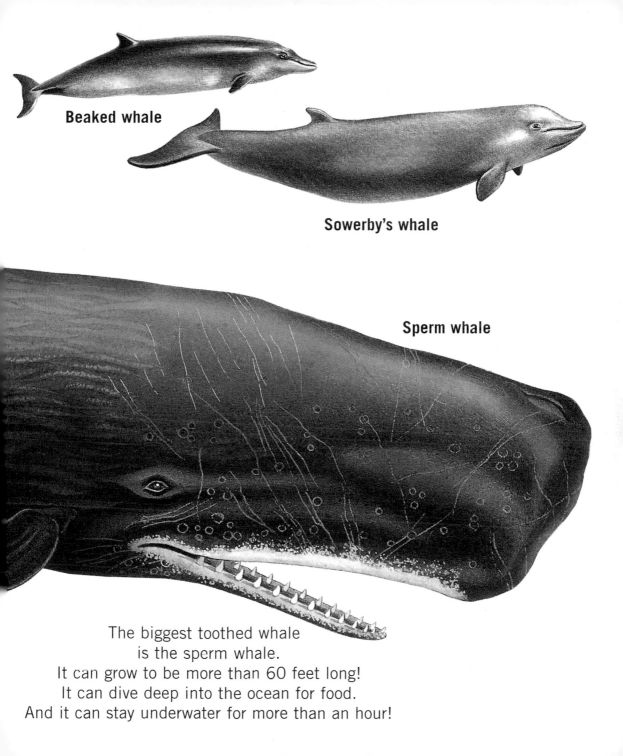

Beaked whale

Sowerby's whale

Sperm whale

The biggest toothed whale
is the sperm whale.
It can grow to be more than 60 feet long!
It can dive deep into the ocean for food.
And it can stay underwater for more than an hour!

Northern right whale

Blue whale

These are baleen whales.
Baleen whales do not have teeth.

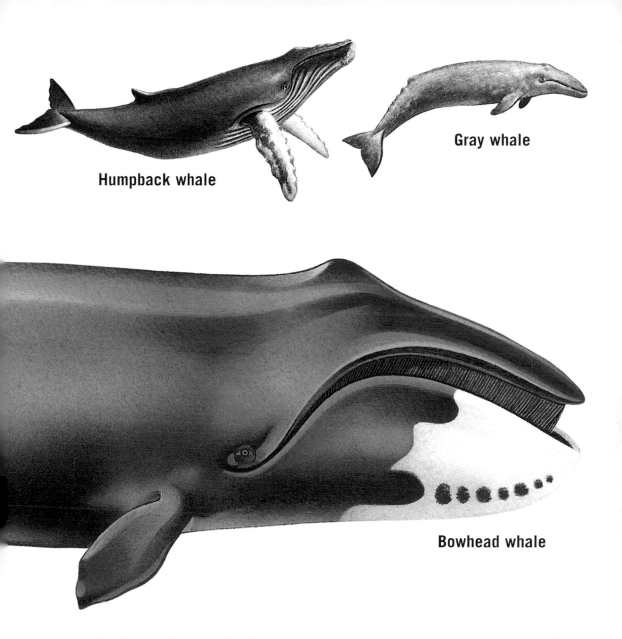

Humpback whale

Gray whale

Bowhead whale

Instead they have baleen, which is like a big comb.
Baleen hangs down from their upper jaw.

Baleen whales use their baleen to catch tiny fish such as krill and plankton.

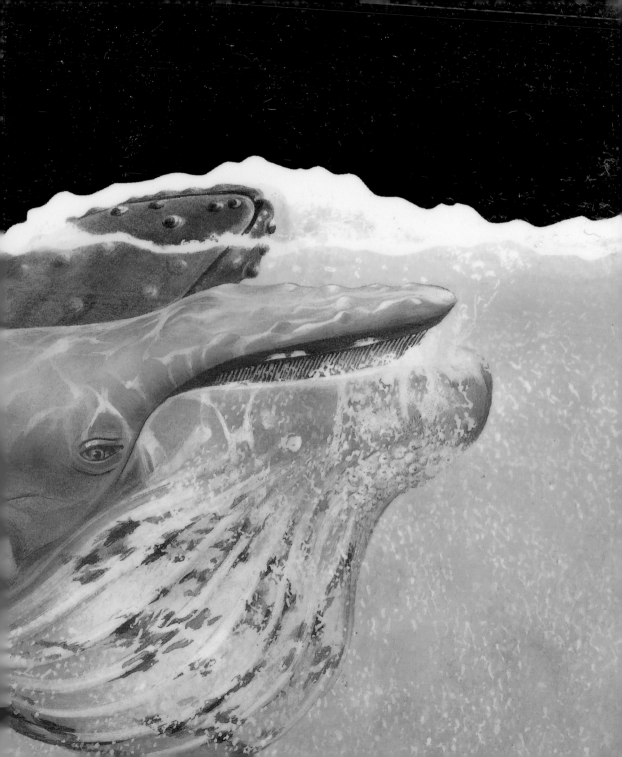

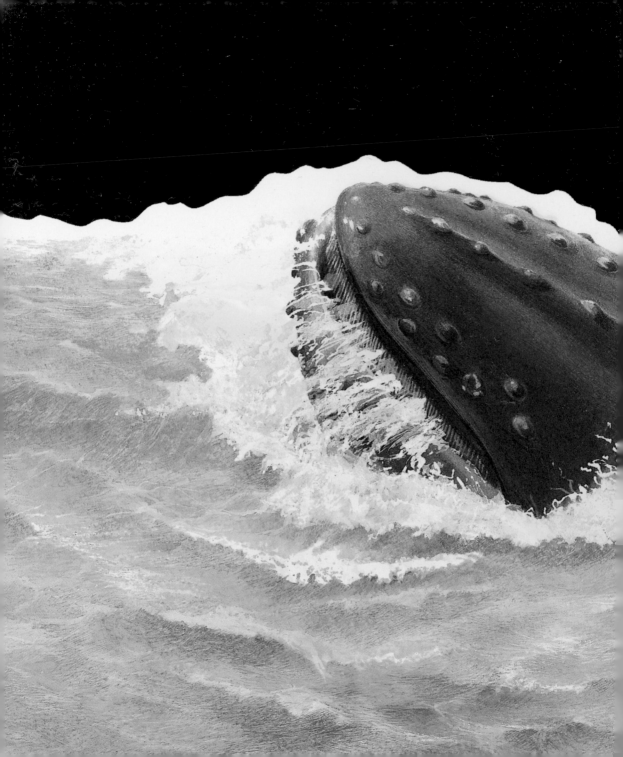

Krill are small, shrimplike animals.
Baleen whales eat up to 8 tons of krill each day.

As the whales swim, they open their mouths.
Fish and water flow in through the baleen.
Then the whale pushes the water back out
through the baleen.
The baleen holds back the fish,
which the whale eats.

Orcas, or killer whales, eat fish,
smaller whales, and penguins.

Orcas are the most ferocious whales.
They hunt as a team and they
share their food.

Orcas knock
over the floating ice.
When the penguins fall
into the water, the orcas
catch a few to eat.

Humpback whales can weigh between 30 to 50 tons!
But they are still able to leap out of the water.

Whales leap to signal danger, to attract a mate, to show off their strength, and just to play.

Female whales give birth to their young in the middle of the ocean, far from shore. Baby whales are called calves.

Female whales help one another deliver their babies.

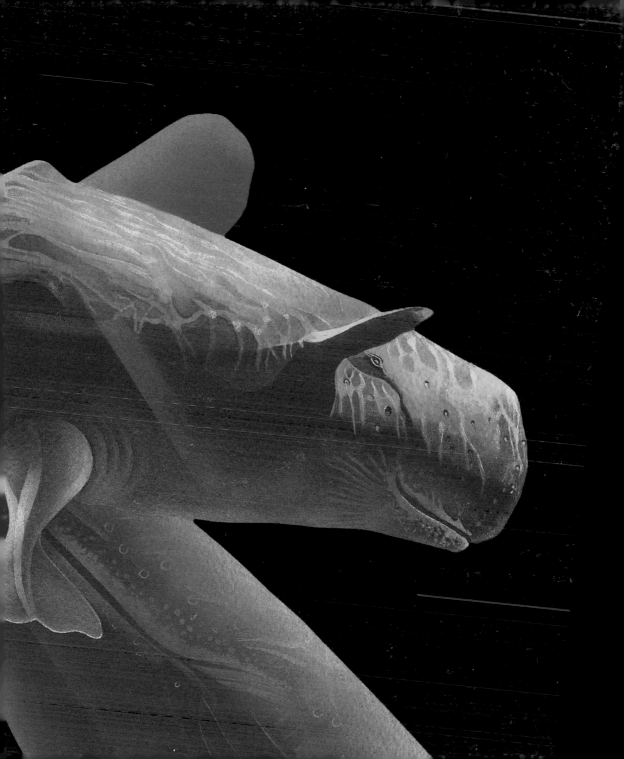

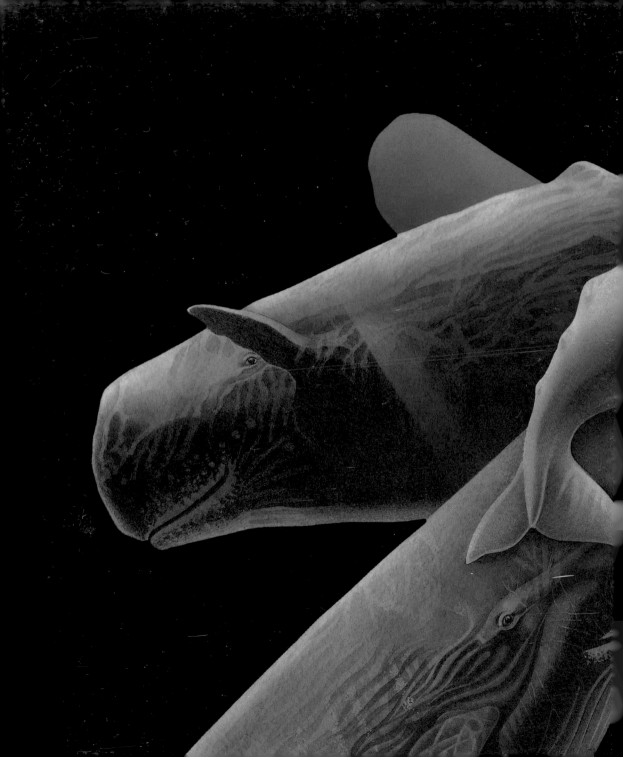

Then the mother lifts
her calf to the surface
of the ocean to breathe.

At sea, fishermen can spot whales
on the horizon by their spray.

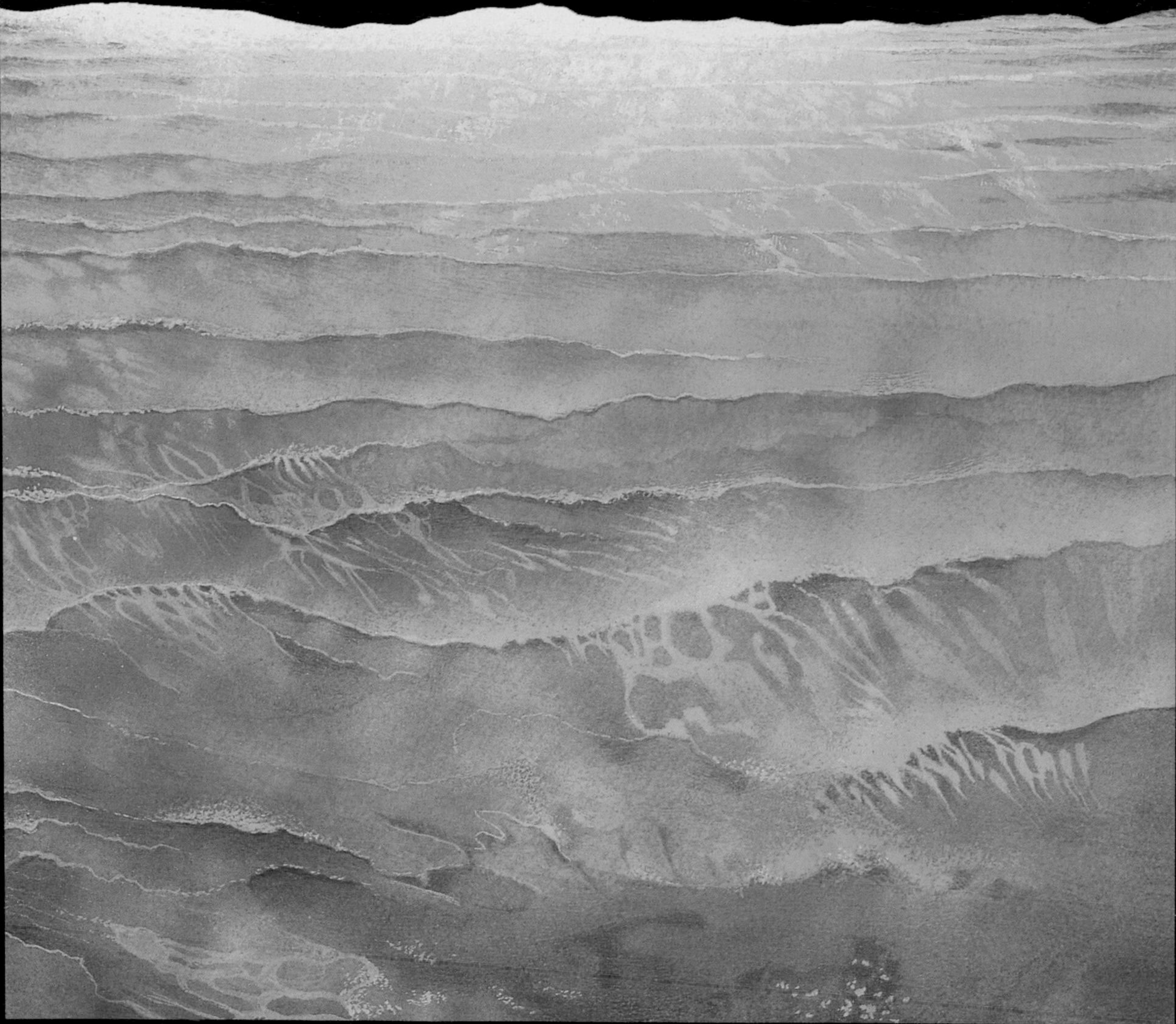

Whales must swim up to the
surface of the ocean to breathe.
Whales breathe through a blowhole
on top of their heads.
When the whale exhales, a spray of
water vapor shoots out!

Many interesting
animals live with the
whales in the deep
waters of the sea.

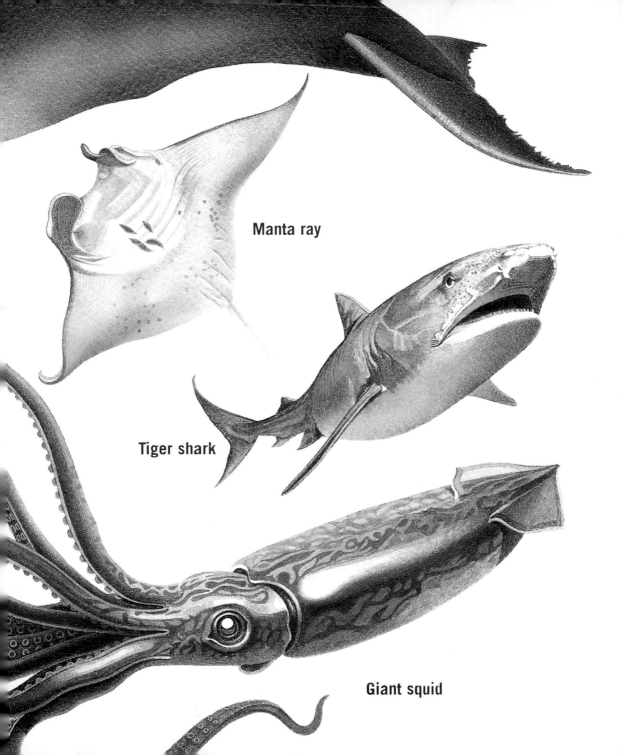

Manta ray

Tiger shark

Giant squid

Striped dolphin

Common dolphin

Dolphins are toothed whales.
Dolphins swim together in groups called pods.

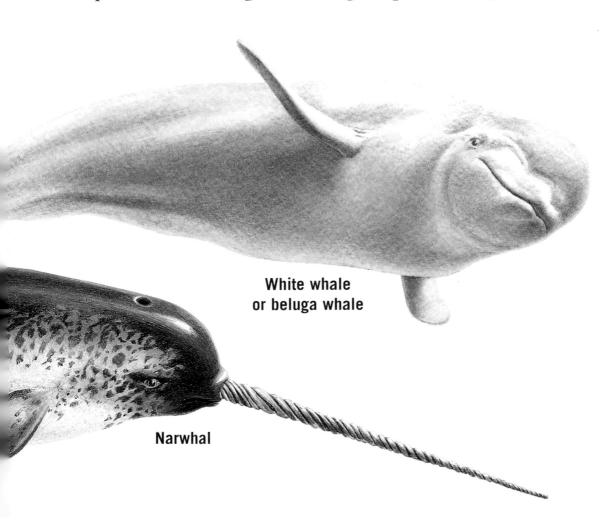

**White whale
or beluga whale**

Narwhal

Here are some other
marine mammals.

Walrus

They also live
in the sea,
but their babies are
born on land.

Sea lion

Seal

The manatee and the
dugong always live in
warm, shallow waters.
Like whales, they
cannot go
on land.

Manatee

Dugong